Calling the Garden from the Grave

poems by

Lesley Clinton

Finishing Line Press
Georgetown, Kentucky

Calling the Garden
from the Grave

Copyright © 2020 by Lesley Clinton
ISBN 978-1-64662-331-0 First Edition
All rights reserved under International and Pan-American Copyright Conventions. No part of this book may be reproduced in any manner whatsoever without written permission from the publisher, except in the case of brief quotations embodied in critical articles and reviews.

ACKNOWLEDGMENTS

Special thanks to the editors of the publications in which these poems first appeared:

2017 Texas Poetry Calendar: "From the Gage Hotel"
By the Light of a Neon Moon, Ed. Janet Lowery. Madville Publishing: "Dancing Before"
Ekstasis Magazine: "Graceless"; "The Sure Roots"
Euphony Journal: "Careful"; "Undying" (as "Latent Strain Waking")
Ever Eden: "New Year Red"
Houston Poetry Fest Anthology: "Hero's Homecoming"; "Contingency" (as "Dirge in Limestone")
Gulf Stream Literary Magazine: "Cabeza de Vaca Weathers the Gulf"
Literary Mama: "If Engulfed" as "What if Engulfed"
Mezzo Cammin: "Rothko Paints the Central Triptych"; "The End of Drehr Avenue"
Sakura Review: "Monologue of the Ghost Tour Guide"
The Windhover: "Keep Watch with Me" (as "Stay Here and Keep Watch with Me")

Publisher: Leah Huete de Maines
Editor: Christen Kincaid
Cover Art: Jacqueline Wind Clinton, artphotography.design
Author Photo: Nicole Early
Cover Design: Elizabeth Maines McCleavy

Order online: www.finishinglinepress.com
also available on amazon.com

Author inquiries and mail orders:
Finishing Line Press
P. O. Box 1626
Georgetown, Kentucky 40324
U. S. A.

Table of Contents

I. A RESTLESS CALLING IN MY ARMS

From the Gage Hotel 1

Dancing Before 2

The Sure Roots 3

Mother's Reply 4

Engulfed 5

Graceless 6

Discernment 7

Contingency 8

Careful 9

II. FILLED WITH UNDYING FIRE

The End of Drehr Avenue 13

Ghost Tour Guide's Monologue 14

Hero's Homecoming 15

Cabeza de Vaca Weathers the Gulf 17

Jacal Mother 18

Rothko Paints the Central Triptych 20

Undying 21

New Year Red 22

Keep Watch with Me 23

The Cathedral Sees Morning 24

Additional Acknowledgments 25

*For Matthew,
Nathaniel,
Connor,
and
Bridget—
my bright callings*

I. A RESTLESS CALLING IN MY ARMS

FROM THE GAGE HOTEL

We walked a bit
to soak in local song

but soon stopped short
when in a velvet sweep

a night train formed:
a metal ghost ship

run off-sea, having found
its rails, riling the stillness,

churning elsewhere's
salt breeze over us,

screeching friction,
pulsing at the joints,

then leaving us
at its wake,

as the restless
often do.

On doldrum nights—
this one, anyway—

I forget my heart
didn't jump on and sail

that steel-forged ambition
over waves of desert.

I startle to find it
still in my chest

DANCING BEFORE

On the midnight prairie, we found
a hall: Tejano and light radiating
from it like a western aurora. Inside,

red Solo cups of Lone Star, large families,
embroidery illuminating
boots and denim. In fact, all

illuminated: smiles, linoleum, fold-out
tables, starched shirts, starry black
hair brushed to the waist.

We danced there, years before children,
to twelve-string fretwork
decadent as fireworks for two.

The singers—their scrollwork harmony
cactus-flower bright.
We saw our someday:

ageless smiles, summer
tracked in on kitchen linoleum, holidays
around fold-out tables, our daughter's

wispy hair, the messy joy
of it, our son's T-shirt covered
with ketchup, all of it. And we knew.

This twelve-string dance meant more—
more dancing,
denim, harmony. All

illuminated.

THE SURE ROOTS

Unkempt, unbridled vine: some days it goes
leggy with wilderness. On other days
it languishes, wilting inside the house.

You find it threaded through thin floorboard cracks
and veined along the undersides of eaves.

It tangles in the junk drawer, twists itself
into the pile of dry-rot rubber bands,
curls around a nail gone white with sheetrock,

no picture now to hang. Although wary
of the order in its tendrils, you tend
it anyway, working in that early
way—with pen, paint, proof, song, or pinch of salt—
to clear a growing space. Soon, leaves unfurl,
gleaming mischief, trekking up barren walls.

To tend a calling means to putter, pore,
tinker, and dive—to lean horizonward,
not sure what fruit waits, dew-still, in the grove
hugging the soul's wild banks. The roots, surely,
have found their reservoir in hallowed ground.

MOTHER'S REPLY

Like holding the horizon close: those nights
in soft-light solitude with you, newborn,
a restless calling in my arms, the heights
and aches ahead uncharted still. I'd torn

my old cares out of me and wished, at least,
you might remember, one day when you'd grown,
our wordless conversations, how we'd speak
in heartbeats. Secret stories, all our own.

I knew one day you'd come to think that I
don't know you, who you've grown to be. And hearts
do come to live in dissonance. That's why
you'll brave these oceaned hopes. That's how it starts:

the dream you shared with me so long ago,
your wordless promise in the nursery glow.

ENGULFED

Sand flecks quiver
in the towel fluff.

Sky-tall from where I lie,
my little one careens
across the soupy sand.

Shoreline shrugging
like a guillotine blade,

the dull sea grins,
bares razor shell shards,
slicks the sand
with spittle.

My boisterous innocent
meets its primordial gaze.

Prey eyeing the lion.

The way it wraps
his ankles
so coolly,
plays piggies with his toes,

the magnificent beast
nearly disarms even me
into thinking

it has been charmed
like some doting auntie, tamed
by this tousled child

who draws in close
then darts back to me, startled
by a clam's dramatic escape.

GRACELESS

Before the surge of gravity
a heady urge wells up—to turn,
to claw the wet, loose-graveled ledge
and scramble back onto its lap.

The air hums with the clarion call
of local kids who've sailed this cliff
all morning—all their lives, in fact—
their dives inscribing splendid arcs

that bend like lavender in wind.
We find our diver in mid-air
for just a fraction of a blink,
two mere, abysmal feet beyond

the cliff, beneath the aqueducts
that have for ages leashed the sky
with pitiless gymnastic grace.
A high-relief of gangliness:

her fingers splayed, her elbows all
rough angles, failing to achieve
with even happenstance good luck
some form that might result

in a smooth meeting with the water
far below. We meet her thus, in sight
of tourists and bronzed locals, dwarfed
by architectural finesse,

maligned by retrospect, a most
distinctive case for study, this
poor victim of mock-epic whim
(her own whim!) finding out firsthand

about the risk in risk-reward,
part one-act improv tragedy
and part postmodern poster child
for acute onset second thought.

DISCERNMENT

You led
   by following. Now I see.

I sought dead ends. You
   threw down your coat.

And I tramped on, unmuddied.
   You deferred, mannered

by some foresight of the way.
   Its rise from the muck.

Its roots muscling
   up from the dirt.

Left to my own myopia—
   tiny empires

puddling
   in my footprint—

I'd still be stuck carving at limestone,
   hands red as a glistening heart,

mad to make it
   (failure on failure)

up some bleak cliff that likely
neither exists nor ends.

CONTINGENCY
Moran Hall of Paleontology, Houston, TX

Here, a fossil drama, cast
in Paleozoic throes.

A horseshoe crab trenched
in mire. Its death march kept

pristine. Arrival nowhere, stamped
with passport surety. The path

a wilting stem, a shoreline snuffed
in sunrise.

Imprinted, framed as specimen,
now millions of years deep

in time's crumbling care.
A creeping, epic end. Of all

earth's poignant subjects, this one
nature labored over, etched in stone.

Survivor, even gone. Flawless
as a David.

CAREFUL

A rare ice day. We tend to things
gone still or stuck, add heat—but slowly,
or a crack might burrow in
and root apart what's whole, reduce
it down to side and side. Night frost
has punched the windshield white. You run
a tepid lip of water
on the glass to clear a vision
of the road ahead. But we don't speak—
words now would bundle cold in cold
or boil too high to safely melt
this opaque distance seizing us.

II. FILLED WITH UNDYING FIRE

THE END OF DREHR AVENUE

$425 a month. Ensconced in trees.
One bedroom, kitchen, bath, and balcony.
The humble luxury of wide baseboards.
A clawfoot tub. Oak floors, a few obscure
planks gone damp. Leafy afternoons with sun-
soaked downpours lending striking lightning views.
A dinner plate perched on one knee, I let
the rainstorms keep me company and found
that seasons steamed with cloud can ravel us
within. Cocooned, we test the lamplit walls.
We're made to weather the inclemency
that drives us. Even embryonic in
my cloistered flat, tucked out of the clouds' reach,
I felt the pressure shift as winter neared.
When boxing up the plates, anthologies,
and sheets, I also packed the thunderbolts,
and I still keep the counsel of those storms.

GHOST TOUR GUIDE'S MONOLOGUE

Voices linger in a place like this.
Mutters roil the air and ooze our names,
distort our waking dreams. But you know
this. You heard the murky lowland call
to you, its words too dense to quite make
out, just faint enough to draw you in.

Down the long bridge, down you drove, bayou
stewing all around, gumming at the ankles
of the past. Now, deep within,
there's this mosquito thrum, this riot.

Here old magic yokes the swarms and slinks
against the cypress trunks. It loiters,
splits raw tallies in the humid boards
of houses shrunk in paint curls. This gray
porch, veiled in fine vacant webs…Picture,
long past, the paint fresh, a hammock draped.

Romantics tend to think they've found some
sultry nook, some summer-thunder,
dog-eared iteration of their lives, but
just remember, ladies, gentlemen:
voices only echo where they're trapped.

HERO'S HOMECOMING
> *Mythology tells us that Aphrodite's priestess Hero followed her lover to a watery death.*

though it's told
she drowned herself

here she sits
salt in her hair

eyes sun-strained
frame in exhale

at the old
table alone

palms face down
she finds the planks

smoother now
each knot somehow

familiar
and unforeseen

damp lung burn
turns to purpose

it feels like
first breath, this turn

a trembling
relief of firsts

with the flushed
oxygen surge

of mission
sweeping in

on the waves' roar
where once blew in

glamour,
with a sailor's ease,

while Hero,
soft as a tongue

of fire kept
in a lantern,

hovered, slight,
at the window

CABEZA DE VACA WEATHERS THE GULF

a worn tide   I retreat
shallows joining the deep
the way life crushes life
thirst malignant in each
arc's rise   sighs in its fall
heartbeats lapping up hours
before fading   obscure
in chambers   empty   full

a crest glossed in sun breeze
I'm no part of the swell
after all   maybe churned
in its maw all this time
but now beaded away
like loose mercury
on a mad roll   sent   exhaled
elemental   airborne

somehow I'm marrow formed
can't go back   not to that
sunken tin soldierhood
that grave   helmeted poise
from my green water caul
I heed the drum   its pulse
writhe self from selfish germ
and rise   go forth   made new

JACAL MOTHER

That first day I bent to look
in the jacal's mouth and saw
we'd have to crouch inside.

I thought of a midwife hunched
there, too. But even then I knew
there'd be no midwife.

—

The boulders seep shadows, bruises
pooling on the land's sunken chest.
We work under hushed cliffs,
hoisting mats of dried ocotillo,
patching holes in the low roof, tending
wounds, adding dirt for weight.

—

Our jacal tucks us under her wing,
and I lie through the night
watching moonlight pass
over the children, skinny limbs
draped in a patchwork of ages

and mothers' bloodlines. The baby
roots for milk. Another labor
gathers within. One day

the stepchildren will whisper
rain and gardens to my babies.
A woman will braid my orphans' hair.

—

The eldest girl chops jicama, humming
with the blade.

The fourth wife's daughter. Now my daughter.

In a year, whose?

Firelight molts our shadows on the rockface.

—

Daybreak. The desert waits, violet.
My farmer unpacks the dry earth for our fall
planting of leather-skinned flat beans.
The sun walks its pure arc over our roof.

—

Boots thud in the corner. Husband
stoops inside out of the wild-winged sunset
and pauses, his eyes accepting the dark.
He moves past me, his palm resting on my belly.

ROTHKO PAINTS THE CENTRAL TRIPTYCH

I sieve lost whispers
from history's throat,
wide, prescient gifts
we have eyes to hear:

the wearing of stone,
geese darkening stars,
the dust of us sifting,
dew starred at our feet,

the frosted breath of
our calling. Mine's the
old wildflower wind that
has tangled the hair

of seekers from all
generations and
borne their yearnings
like dandelion seeds

bound for soil or stone.
I mean to take part
in the visceral blare
of moment, to sing

with mute pigments
to my vacancy
and yours—lurking, too—
the first of all songs

in language that can't
grow stale or go lost.
For this I still redden
each abyss a tinge.

UNDYING

All gleam and teeth,
the Milky Way slices the darkness.
The final man and woman
have come to the desert floor
to hear their ancestors' echoes.

Bleached bones like runes
glow silver under cool night,
riddle at some hidden ingress.

His jaw a taut bowstring,
her eyes chiseled flint,
she turns to him. Survival on his breath,
he exhales into her hair, a gesture
wholly human—the last of such,
of saying, wanting to say.

Their veins teem with a drive to build,
to knead from the sand one last civilization
even as the foundation caves—

for something always lasts,
wears marked change.
Deep in the wayfaring canyon,
all ache and urgency,
they plot transit between potentials.

They've read their fate—
blood, decay, re-formation—
but still chart the abyss undaunted.
They are a spark from an eternal hearth.

Suns blear in the falling sky. Burn
cold. Lie in wait for the spark to land,
and tense for the bright reply.

NEW YEAR RED

Her mother sent it with a note about the fit.
After two alterations it was still tight,

which she'd never say, but Mom would see
on Skype and would point out in her advice voice.

At the Tết dinner it would be
Mom is well, yes. Sends hugs,

the whole time, no doubt, to friends and neighbors
in clothes like petals after rain. Flashing smiles.

Drums. Dragons. Red áo dài[1]. Red lips. Red envelopes,
one tucked in the folded silk. Inside, a tuition check.

And at home, mom's lips are pale and her bones
porous and she is filled with undying fire.

It fuels her—to sew care out of
nothing, to make all who know her rich

as the silk of the New Year áo dài, preciously folded
and borne on wings across the world to daughter.

---

1 An *áo dài* is a traditional Vietnamese garment often worn on festive occasions like Tết, the Lunar New Year.

KEEP WATCH WITH ME

A long match smokes, the hot end quiet now,
gone crisp and gray. Behind, a choir of flames
makes harmony of light and gleams the names
of loved ones lost. There, on the bottom row:
a quarter lit the wick that bears my prayer
and keeps late watch with me. But fire dies out.
This kneeler's worn with centuries of doubt.
How will one dim, soft drop of firelight fare
in loss this cavernous? Ghosts slip back through
the noose. My skeletons shadow around.
One tea light can't illuminate profound
despair. The warmth burns low and pales to blue,
and as the small flame leaves me at wick's end,
the faintest chord of dawn sings soft *amen*.

THE CATHEDRAL SEES MORNING

Her saints' faces flayed long ago,
the molasse belle on the near bank
bears the past like a brittle scroll.

Certain blocks high in her façade
seek daylight with empty sockets—
remnants of a graveyard origin—

carved by Gallo-Roman hands
so, on ancestral days, the living
could break wine-soaked bread

with the dead. Was it a hopeful act?
To lift those stones up heavenward?
For this is no mausoleum.

Webbed windows, ashen without,
blazon gem-bright news within.
Through the triumphs and agonies

dawn reaches into the hush
where *mea culpas* sigh
up alcove walls. Bouquet rays

gather at the knees of the found,
petaled in hair, on folds of clothes,
calling the garden up out of the grave.

Additional Acknowledgments

Thanks to those who helped this collection bloom by offering feedback on poems, mentoring with publication advice, or allowing me to share this work with a broader audience. I'm especially grateful to John Barone; Kim Bridgford; Sarah Cortez; Maria Illich; Jeff Johnson, S.J.; Janet Lowery; Larry W. Massey, Jr.; Mark McNeil; Lisa Salinas; Herman Sutter; Sally Thomas; my insightful Strake Jesuit Students; and my sunny, supportive family.

Lesley Clinton has won awards from the Poetry Society of Texas and Press Women of Texas. She has been a Juried Poet at the Houston Poetry Fest three times and in 2019 received the Lucille Johnson Clarke Memorial award. Her poetry and prose have appeared in publications such as *America Magazine, Mezzo Cammin, The Windhover, Texas Poetry Calendar, Ever Eden, Ekstasis Magazine, Radiant Magazine, Sakura Review, Literary Mama, Euphony Journal, Gulf Stream Magazine,* and *By the Light of a Neon Moon*. Lesley teaches at Strake Jesuit College Preparatory and has a Master of Arts in Teaching. She serves as a board member of Catholic Literary Arts in the greater Houston area, where she lives with her husband and three children. Visit her at lesleyclinton.com.

www.ingramcontent.com/pod-product-compliance
Lightning Source LLC
LaVergne TN
LVHW041511070426
835507LV00012B/1480